Who Can Fly?

By CODY MCKINNEY

Illustrated by MAXINE LEE

CANTATA
LEARNING
MANKATO, MINNESOTA

CANTATA
LEARNING

MANKATO, MINNESOTA

Published by Cantata Learning
1710 Roe Crest Drive
North Mankato, MN 56003
www.cantatalearning.com

Library of Congress Control Number: 2014938315
ISBN: 978-1-63290-075-3

Who Can Fly? by Cody McKinney
Illustrated by Maxine Lee

Book design by Tim Palin Creative
Music produced by Wes Schuck
Audio recorded, mixed, and mastered at Two Fish Studios, Mankato, MN

Printed in the United States of America.

VISIT
WWW.CANTATALEARNING.COM/ACCESS-OUR-MUSIC

Have you ever wished you could fly like a bird?

There are many different kinds of birds. They come in many colors and sizes. Listen and learn about the wild world of birds!

5

When you look up in the sky
and see the wings just floating by,
don't you wish you were a bird?

You could fly.

6

Birds are found most everywhere,
from Timbuktu to Kalamazoo to Delaware.

Their house is a nest up in a tree made out of sticks.

They raise their chicks so one day they'll be able to fly.

Many birds are **predators** that hunt for food.

A penguin lives on ice that makes him one cool dude.

They swim around the ocean with their flippers and wings.

And huddle all together to keep warm, but what they can't do is fly.

11

When birds **migrate**, they fly in a "V"
over a **habitat** of trees
to a warm, sunny place to have their babies
hatch out their eggs, not like you,
not like me.

They **nurse** them up strong,
carry food in their beak (mostly worms).

And a day will come when the chicks are not
weak. And they can fly.

There are black ones, yellow ones, brown ones, too.

They molt their feathers and look real cool.

Some are the predators, and some are **prey**.

They never need a taxi at the end of the day. They can fly.

Certain birds can live to over 30 years.

That's a lot of time to put into the birdie career.

Some bigger birds: the albatross, the eagle, and Larry.

A woodpecker has feathers, but some of them are hairy. Why?

The seagulls they play on the sandy **dunes**.

They might take your lunch, but they'll sing you a tune.

And a parrot can talk like a regular guy.

And buffalo wings are just chicken wings fried. And birds can fly.

BREAD CRUMBS

So when you see a bird up high,

you might know which one passed you by.

Then you close your eyes and dream.

You can fly.

GLOSSARY

dune—a hill or ridge of sand piled up by the wind

habitat—the natural place and conditions in which a plant or animal lives

Larry—as in Larry Bird, a famous basketball player who played for the Boston Celtics; his number was 33.

migrate—to move from one place to another

nurse—to treat with care

predator—an animal that hunts other animals for food

prey—an animal hunted by another animal for food

Who Can Fly?

Cody McKinney

Pop Ballad

When you look in – to the sky..........................

and see the wings..... just floa – ting by.............................

Don't you wish...... you were a.................. bird?............................ You could

fly...

ACTIVITY

1. Not all birds fly. In this song there are penguins, which can't fly. Can you think of other birds that are unable fly?

2. Draw your own bird!

3. What does your bird eat?

4. Where does your bird live?

5. How does your bird travel to different places?

6. What color is your bird?

7. Name your bird!

TO LEARN MORE

Crupi, Jaclyn. *Not All Birds Fly*. Engage Literacy. Mankato, MN: Capstone Classroom, 2013.

Nelson, Robin. *Migration*. First Step Nonfiction. Discovering Nature's Cycles. Minneapolis: Lerner, 2011.

Olien, Rebecca. *Where Do the Birds Go?: A Migration Mystery*. First Graphics. Mankato, MN: Capstone Press, 2012.

Veitch, Catherine. *Bird Babies*. Acorn. Mankato, MN: Capstone Press, 2014.